D0982616

WHAT SHOULD PARENTS EXPECT?

WHAT SHOULD PARENTS EXPECT?

John M. Drescher

Abingdon

Nashville

WHAT SHOULD PARENTS EXPECT?

Copyright © 1980 by Abingdon

Library of Congress Cataloging in Publication Data

DRESCHER, JOHN M
  What should parents expect.
  Bibliography: p. 90
  1. Parenting—United States.   2.   Moral education—United
  States.   I.   Title.
  HQ755.85.D73   261.8'342'7   79-20949

ISBN 0-687-44909-X

MANUFACTURED BY THE PARTHENON PRESS AT
NASHVILLE, TENNESSEE, UNITED STATES OF AMERICA

CONTENTS

Preface

This year millions of people will take a step which will significantly change their lives and in addition the lives of future generations. They will become parents. How they rear their children will determine the destiny of nations more than national leadership, modern technology, and art.

One concern parents around the world share in common is how to instill in their children the values, ideals, and motivation which will help them to know not only right from wrong but also to make responsible and right decisions. How do we teach obedience and responsibility? How can we instill a healthy independence? Does a child perceive authority differently at different ages? Are there different approaches to teach at appropriate times?

In recent years extensive research offers practical guidance for parents to help children develop a moral

7

sense. Research, recognizing that children differ in their development, finds that there are certain critical periods in the child's life when a particular kind of guidance is needed. It is helpful to know what to expect of children at various ages in behavior and achievement.

Several things appear clear. One is that many children are pushed into roles before they are ready for them. Much undue pressure is put on children to cease being children. Norman Vincent Peale says that parents must beware of making children ego-props or trying to stamp them into molds which suit the parents best. He also points out that parents can treat children as extensions of themselves instead of letting them be persons in their own rights. This leads to crushing failures in parent-child relationships.

The first section deals with this concern.

A second thing continues clear. Parents are the primary and most important persons to teach moral values to children. A Harvard study shows that the influence of other agencies, such as school and church, depends chiefly on those characteristics the child already carries with him from home. Parents, whether they realize it or not, teach moral values everyday.

Dr. Carl Rutt, adult and child psychiatrist, said to a medical group meeting near Pittsburgh, Pennsylvania: "Most of what I've learned in life, which is of value, I've learned from my parents. And I've told them so. They did not read a lot of books on raising children, but they taught us the basic values of life." Parents are teaching all the time either by default or by decision.

It is during the early years in the family that the child learns the inner controls that determine behavior. A young mother once asked her minister when she should begin training her son for God. The minister asked, "How old is your son?" She said her son was just five. Then he replied,

"Begin immediately. You have already missed five of the best years."

This small book is by no means exhaustive. It does not discuss in detail the ten or more stages of development and the characteristics of each. This book looks at several broad stages which will give parents understanding and guidance. Few parents need to be reminded that children vary greatly, and so the time of their application of different principles will, of necessity, also vary.

This book does not use technical language. It is not written for scholars who have numerous books of research using technical terms at their fingertips. Rather, the attempt here is to take advantage of much which has been studied in such research and to share it with the average parent, so that those at the job of raising children can find help and hope.

Love of the child will always be a primary need, but in child-rearing, love is not the only requisite for parenthood. The child needs a love that carries a special kind of insight into his own world, that feeds his spirit, and that gives him the psychic strength to build firm concepts about himself and life around him. He needs also the kind of moral guidance that will give him a sense of responsibility and reverance to make right decisions.

Note: In this book *he, him,* and *his* are used in the established sense, when appropriate, as pronouns of the common gender to include the male and the female. Since gender is a category of grammar rather than sex, the use of the already existing distinction is made solely in the interest of clarity and economy of language.

Father Forgets

Listen, son: I am saying this as you lie asleep, one little paw crumpled under your cheek and the blond curls stickily wet on your damp forehead. I have stolen into your room alone. Just a few minutes ago as I sat reading my paper in the library, a stifling wave of remorse swept over me. Guiltily I came to your bedside.

These are the things I was thinking, son: I had been cross to you. I scolded you as you were dressing for school because you gave your face merely a dab with a towel. I took you to task for not cleaning your shoes. I called out angrily when you threw some of your things on the floor.

At breakfast I found fault, too. You spilled things. You gulped down your food. You put your elbows on the table. You spread butter too thick on your bread. And as you started off to play and I made for my train, you turned and waved a hand and called, "Good-bye, Daddy!" and I frowned, and said in reply, "Hold your shoulders back!"

Then it began all over again in the late afternoon. As I came up the road I spied you, down on your knees, playing marbles. There were holes in your stockings. I humiliated you before your boy friends by marching you ahead of me to the house. Stockings were expensive—and if you had to buy them you would be careful! Imagine that, son, from a father!

Do you remember, later, when I was reading in the library, how you came in, timidly, with a sort of hurt look in your eyes? When I glanced up over my paper, impatient at the interruption, you hesitated at the door. "What is it you want?" I snapped.

You said nothing, but ran across in one tempestuous plunge, and threw your arms around my neck and kissed me, and your small arms tightened with an affection that God had set blooming in your heart and which even neglect could not wither. And then you were gone, pattering up the stairs.

Well, son, it was shortly afterward that my paper slipped from my hands and a terrible sickening fear came over me. What has habit been doing to me? The habit of finding fault, of reprimanding—this was my reward to you for being a boy. It was not that I did not love you; it was that I expected too much of you. I was measuring you by the yardstick of my own years.

And there was so much that was good and fine and true in your character. The little heart of you was as big as the dawn itself over the wide hills. This was shown by your spontaneous impulse to rush in and kiss me good night. Nothing else matters tonight, son. I have come to your bedside in the darkness, and I have knelt there, ashamed!

It is a feeble atonement; I know you would not understand these things if I told them to you during your waking hours. But tomorrow I will be a real daddy! I will chum with you, and suffer when you suffer, and laugh when you laugh. I will bite my tongue when impatient words come. I will keep saying as if it were a ritual: "He is nothing but a boy—a little boy!"

I am afraid I have visualized you as a man. Yet as I see you now, son, crumpled and weary in your cot, I see that you are still a baby. Yesterday you were in your mother's arms, your head on her shoulder. I have asked too much, too much.

—W. Livingston Larned

Do you expect your child to perform better than other children? Are you pushing him too hard to reach unnatural and impossible high standards? The child who falls short of such standards may only feel inferior and so retreat into his own world.

Encourage your child's small successes. His ego thrives on approval, success, and achievement that is within his range of ability.

Go easy on criticism. Some parents, anxious to rear a perfect child, criticize too freely and overwork the nos and the don'ts. They find, then, that they have raised a child who is always ill at ease and hesitant, and who draws back from any kind of action or decision.—Gertrude Karafa

The Demise of Childhood

I was seated in the third row watching a wrestling tournament. The tournament was provided by the community during the summer months for the grade-school students. The boys had practiced for some weeks, and now they were in the finals. Parents and friends were present. Excitement was high.

A little fellow, perhaps nine years old, had just finished and lost his match. Dejectedly he walked over and sat beside his father in front of me. To my dismay the father began to deride and criticize, even curse, his small son for his failure to win.

His son sat silent and still as he suffered, not only what was a humiliating defeat before so many adults, but also, even worse, a pitiless onslaught by his own father in front of others. He suffered all this from a supposedly grown-up man who somehow felt the important thing was winning, from a parent who found his own ego hurt or threatened when his son failed to win.

What does an incident like this say? It is only one illustration of our failure to let children be children. Even more, it is an example of how we as parents seek to find our own fulfillment in our children. Children in our society are under tremendous pressure to succeed beyond their years. And the success aimed for is usually that of the parents rather than that of the children.

Eberhard Arnold in his excellent book *Children's Education in Community: The Basis of Bruderhof Education,* writes: "If we exploit the child's ability to devote himself to something great by binding him to ourselves and to our own little ego . . . or to selfish gratification, we are corrupting the child and destroying his childlike spirit." [1]

Let Children Be Children

Children have the right to be immature and to be permitted to grow up gradually. Our children need from us the opportunity for experiences that they are capable of handling, our assurance that we are there to encourage them, and our acceptance of their efforts without belittling them.

The soaring suicide rate among adolescents confirms that childhood is not a happy time. Dr. E. James Anthony, St. Louis psychoanalyst, points out that today's children appear to be born old. Their faces are cynical as they enter adolescence. The reasons, Anthony says, are that we as parents expect too much too soon, and particularly the middle-class parents are pushing their offspring to accomplish. Children are under sustained pressure.

Dr. James Dobson, assistant professor of pediatrics at the University of Southern California School of Medicine and director of behavior research, Division of Child Development, for Children's Hospital of Los Angeles, writes in *Hide or Seek*, "The current epidemic of self-doubt has resulted from a totally unjust and unnecessary system of evaluating human worth now prevalent in our society." He devotes two chapters to an analysis of the false values on which self-esteem so often depends in our culture. The two he discusses in depth are beauty and intelligence. Beauty and brains seem to be prime requisites, if one is to be of any worth.

According to Martha Weinman Lear, author of *The Child Worshipers*, the younger generation is our most reliable status symbol. The hopes, dreams, and ambitions of the entire family sometimes rest on the shoulders of an immature child. And in the atmosphere of fierce competition in which we place the child, he is severely damaged.

In an article in *U. S. Catholic*, "Let My Children Grow," Ned O'Gorman writes: "I know a boy of six who wrote a poem about his perception of life, and one line in it was: 'School is a closed door.' I think there are children who might write: 'Childhood is a closed door.' And when they are older might add: 'Childhood is a closed door. My parents and teachers closed it.' "[2]

Armin Grams in *The Christian Encounters; Changes in Family Life* says that "paradoxically, the child-centered home has brought with it unprecedented pressures for children to stop being children. We have taken childhood away from children, not only by watching them too closely and focusing on them excessively. We are also unwilling to permit them their time in growing up."[3]

What Do We Do?

Because we do not see childhood as a legitimate phase of life itself, and because we as parents feel the need to find our success in our children, we do many ridiculous things.

At three months we buy toys parents like to play with. An electric train is purchased and set up by parents whose child still wants to stack blocks. A tricycle stands riderless with the driver still in diapers. We dress five-year-olds in caps and gowns for kindergarten graduation. A little fellow recently said, "I think it is bad I graduated because I can't even read."

Little girls who desire to play with dolls are driven downtown for dancing lessons. We pair boys and girls off in first grade. We elect them to class offices before they have an idea what it means. We form committees and teach them to vie for position before they know what a committee is. We dress them like adults. And some mothers are proud when their eleven- and twelve-year-old daughters are popular with the boys. "Little Miss" and beauty contests are held, paying undue and the wrong kind of attention to children.

In sports we expect children to play like professionals before they have hips big enough to hold up their uniforms and before they have hands large enough to handle a ball and glove. And while the game is going on, parents sit on the sidelines harassing the player who makes a mistake, applauding the one who excels, and yelling for victory at all costs. Some time ago a little-league coach told me that parents should not be allowed to come to games. Adults spoil the fun. They will not allow children to enjoy the game as children.

Little leagues often deny the child the right to be a child. First, there is too much pressure for him to produce while adults cheer or criticize, depending on how adult the performance is. Second, the whole setting is unchildlike in that only the good players play, and the creativity of learning through failure in a loving atmosphere is missing. Then, too, the game must be played according to adult rules and supervised by adult coaches and umpires.

Parents drive children to despair in their demand to make good grades. And it is not uncommon for children to say that they cheated because of pressure from parents.

Even in the church, mothers and fathers sometimes feel the church is neglecting, even rejecting, them as parents if the church bulletin or announcement misses calling attention to accomplishments of their child. If the church fails to use their child prodigy in singing or other performances, some parents are hurt. Our precious children are put forward to place feathers in our caps.

Our vocabulary says we are geared, not to children, but to later years. We speak of preschool, preadolescence, preteens, and junior high school. Even the preadolescent bra has good sales.

In an article, "No Furniture Till Forty," Phyllis Naylor says we should have the type of furniture in our homes that allow children freedom in playing. If we must continually tell children to take their hands off things, it is likely that we have our priorities in the wrong place. Things, rather than persons, predominate in our thinking.

Marilyn Bonham in *Laughter and Tears of Children* points out that parents and society contribute to precocious sexuality. Dating of nine- or ten-year-olds is considered right by some parents. The twelve-year-old is often provoked into a sexual identification that is far too premature and probably not of the child's design in the first place. So also, Bonham points out, "The premature use of lipstick, nail polish, teased hair, and high heels is psychologically unsound and denies the child the all-too-brief innocence of childhood."[4]

Some fathers push sons into all kinds of situations of masculine independence and thus hamper the emotional growth of a child who is still floundering about in search of himself.

Behavioral scientists are telling us that toy manufacturers and other business interests are being successful in changing the nature of children's play. Instead of three- and four-year-olds playing with stuffed animals or dolls, trucks or model cars, they are pushed to fantasize about life as an adolescent. Just one example is the Barbie Doll that centers on sex and materialism.

Because of such pressures psychiatrists warn that children are breaking down in increasing numbers and at younger and younger ages. The great drive for superiority builds all kinds of feelings of inferiority. And feelings of inferiority make up the number-one emotional problem of teen-agers today, a problem that drives many to depend on drugs and drink.

At least two things force these feelings of inferiority. The great stress on our children to be superior, of course, builds all kinds of feelings of inadequacy. Few can be superior in one thing. How much less can a child be superior in many things? Another reason for the inferiority complex, the number-one problem of teen-agers today, is the overly permissive home that forces youth to make decisions they are not ready to make because of lack of experience and knowledge. When parents are not standing by to assist youth in the decisions of life and have no clear code of conduct themselves, they are bound to build feelings of insecurity in their children.

What's Back of It?

We must ask the question, Why do parents put so much pressure on their children to excel in beauty and brains, in sports and showmanship, and in dressing and performing beyond their age?

Is it that the childlike qualities of imperfection, curiosity, honesty, and naivete are threatening to parents? Is it that parents are so insecure that any failure on the part of the child threatens them?

Is it that we get our ego trips from our children? We strive to succeed through our children. We get a vicarious experience through what our children accomplish. Perhaps we have failed in accomplishing what we desire, so we must have children who succeed at all costs. Seeing our children in proper focus is difficult if we are unhappy in our own lives.

Psychiatrist Bernard Trossman has said that perhaps the most deleterious parental attitude is the spoken or unspoken communication that the child must provide meaning for the parents' empty lives.

When a mother pushes her daughter into beauty contests, or a dad pressures his son into sports or some academic endeavor, or a parent places the birthday picture of their two-year-old in the newspaper, are they concerned for the child, or are they only getting their own ego trip from it all?

Might the pressure we put on our children be at times the result of our having set impossible standards of achievement for ourselves? The result is that we make excessive demands on our children. We burden our children with our expectations for achievement because of our own feelings of inadequacy.

Is There a Remedy?

Sometimes parents feel forced into allowing children to enter into roles far too early by the standards others set. Gene Church Schulz, a teacher and an astute observer of youth, wrote an article in which she states that young people "need parents who are strong enough to stem the rising tide of growing up too soon." She describes the difficulty of being the "heavy" in the drama of growing up. The older youngsters become, the louder they may cry that "everybody else is doing it." Parties last too long, boy-girl affairs start before children are ready, and all kinds of grown-up situations are forced on adolescents. She points out that it is very easy to let children follow the practice of the crowd, to bend with the prevailing wind, to say, "Oh, I suppose so—this time."

"However," says teacher Schultz, "there is another consideration. When parents band together in organizations like the Parents' League or even informal groups, the position of each is strengthened. Usually other parents share our concern. They would like to say 'no,' but lack the muscle to enforce it. A single phone call to another pair of parents may bring in reinforcements."

We must examine our family values. What are our real concerns? If our values are so low that getting ahead materially, being popular, and receiving applause are first, then we will go on using our children, and we will place primary emphasis on things rather than on persons. To see our children clearly we must examine our own values, goals, and attitudes, and look at ourselves as parents.

In an article, "Who Is Pressuring Pre-schoolers?" James L. Hymes, Jr., writes: "Parents are trapped by their love for their children. They don't pressure them because they are callous or careless; parents pressure because they care. They want their youngsters to have the best, to be the best, to know the best, to do the best. Their fond wishes and their aspirations, their hopes and their dreams, not to mention their own pressures, drive them—and they drive their youngsters."[5]

However, steady pressure strains life and presents the constant possibility of failure for the child. It takes the joy out of living. Steady pressure is bound to strike at personal worth and dignity. It says, "You don't measure up." It leads to rejection later of even good standards, when the pressure can no longer be applied in adolescence or when leaving home for college or work.

But as a parent we do not need to stay trapped in driving ourselves or our children. We can stand back and consider what counts most in life, what is most important. We can look at what we really want. We do not need to make our children pawns of our unfilled personal needs or dreams.

We must stop robbing our children of happiness by forcing them into roles for which they are not yet ready. The parent who allows for creativity on the part of the child and stands by when the child does his best, even though he has failed, will have a child who will develop confidence and trust, a child who will find life an open, happy experience. Children need understanding as they use their resources to develop a sense of fulfillment through the imagination, curiosity, and wonder of childhood.

All this does not mean that parents should drop all aspirations for their children and do nothing. It does not mean that we let our child do as he wills. It means rather that we look closely at our motives and aspirations and recognize them for what they are. It means that we consider carefully what things help most in developing our child into a free, independent, and responsible adult.

When loving parents spend time with the child, they are doing the best teaching. Skills grow best in good, happy relationships. And when time is spent listening, answering questions, working and playing together, a lot can happen. When loving parents do things with their child and go places together, the best creative happenings can occur. When there are story times, game times, fun times, talking times, the parents are opening all kinds of doors the child will be happy to walk through rather than be pushed through. And when he walks through doors out of his own desire, he is participating as a happy, responsible, and patient person rather than fulfilling a role for which he is not ready.

Dr. Bernie Wiebe writes how, through a mistake made on a citizen's list in Houston, Texas, a two-year-old child received a summons for jury duty. Says Wiebe: "To me that seems like a double ironic error. First, here we again see a child cast into the role of an adult. But it should perhaps remind us that the child is a legitimate judge before which civilization should be tested."[6]

Discussion Statements and Questions

1. Do you agree with the basic idea that we do not let children be children?
2. Discuss other ways we put pressure on children to be adults.
3. Sports is always a touchy subject in this discussion. What do you think of spectator sports for young children?

4. Discuss the great drive for superiority that builds all kinds of feelings of inferiority.
5. Discuss additional reasons why we put pressure on children to excel.
6. In your mind what can parents do to turn the trend away from using children for their own ego trips?

Research in the field of education has pointed out that a child's first and most important teachers are his parents, especially his mother. Another noteworthy finding is that a child's most significant intellectual, emotional, and social learnings take place during the earlier years of childhood. Never again, in such a short period of time, can one hope to influence a person so greatly.—Neal Buchanan

If I were asked what single qualification was necessary for one who has the care of children, I should say patience—patience with their tempers, with their understandings, with their progress. It is not brilliant parts or great acquirements which are necessary for teachers, but patience to go over first principles again and again, steadily to add a little everyday: never to be irritated by willful or accidental hindrance.—Fenelon

Of nineteen out of twenty things in children, take no special notice; but if, as to the twentieth you give a direction or command see that you are obeyed.—Tryon Edwards

A three-year-old was talking animatedly to her mother. The mother stared ahead, silent—until suddenly she exploded, her voice furious, detonating. "That's all I ever get from you! Chatter, chatter, chatter!" The little girl's lively, intelligent face changed, and she looked away, self-conscious, off balance, and silly. I wondered what else a mother expected to get from a three-year-old. What else has a small child to give? And what gift could one have that is more tender, more joyous, more remarkable?—A friend

Age of Regulation— Birth to Age Seven

"No man ever wetted clay and left it, as if there would be bricks by chance and fortune."—Plutarch

A second-grade girl shared the day's activities at school with her mother. "We had a substitute teacher at school today," she said. "She let us do anything we wanted to, and we didn't like her."

This comment carries within itself both the response and need of a child during the early years, particularly from birth through age seven. While it is true the older child desires and needs clear controls to be content and secure, the fact is that, in a special way, in the early years of childhood, the child needs to know what is expected. Regulation speaks of rules. And the child without rules becomes unruly. He also becomes unhappy, insecure, and develops feelings of not being loved. Further, he will kick out, sometimes in very annoying ways, to feel where his boundaries of control are.

The Prime Years

These early years of childhood are the prime years in the child's moral development. He needs to know what he *ought* to do before he can think or practice what he *should* do. This learning begins at birth and will be learned primarily from those closest to him, hopefully from loving and caring parents.

As the child comes into the home dependent on parents for physical and emotional nourishment and development, he comes also dependent on parents for the development of his moral character. There is no better time to teach obedience, which is the first element in the development of a conscience and moral sense, than the first years. The Bible and the best psychologists agree in telling us that the training of the child in the way he should go is the parents' responsibility. This training begins early and helps determine the direction of the child for the rest of his life.

Behavioral patterns, acquired early, stay with the child. Good habits become worthy character. Bad habits produce undesirable character. Aristotle refers to this, "That which has become habitual becomes as it were, a part of our nature." And good habits give a person the freedom to deal with life's problems and save him from a haphazard and frustrated later life.

During the early years the child develops a constellation of attitudes, values, and emotional responses that determine his direction and choices for life. These first impressions and experiences are deep and lasting. From the earliest moments parents are molding for the years ahead. These basic attitudes will undergo change with each new experience, but the fundamental character will persist. He may see himself as a responsible person with the right to exist, or he may see himself as a nobody who must always apologize for being alive. He may see his parents as godlike figures who must be always right, or he may see them as fallible human beings who struggle to protect and nurture him according to their abilities and insights.

"Not only does his sense of being a person develop out of his relationship with other persons, but the kind of person he judges himself to be will depend on the kind of persons he is with and the way in which they feel about him and treat him. The first three years of a child's life are acutely important for his development as a person."[1]

This reflection, which the child sees of himself as he looks at the reaction of others toward him, is sometimes spoken of as the "looking-glass self." This is how the child picks up ideas about himself that say he is good or bad, strong or weak, kind or mean, worthy or worthless, likable or unlikable, trustworthy or untrustworthy, friendly or unfriendly, courageous or cowardly, honest or dishonest, beautiful or ugly.

It is necessary to insert some caution into the many statements concerning the early years of childhood being the most formative years. We must beware of a determinism that leaves little or no place for the child's personal choices and other influences on the child later in life.

A few years ago, some espoused a deterministic philosophy, which circulated such slogans as, "Give me a child until he is three, and you can have him for the rest of his life," or "Train a child properly or fail to train the child properly the first few years and you determine his future." In some circles this determinism is still propagated. Such statements do not consider the many Christian teachings concerning change, and they leave parents with a sense of hopelessness and despair. In addition they take away personal responsibility, personal choice, and freedom. It would seem that the importance of the early years can be fully stressed without this deterministic outlook.

To say that the early years are especially important in shaping the future does not mean that if a parent does everything exactly right, the child no longer has a choice and must turn out right in each detail. God does everything right and for the good of his children, yet not everyone responds and chooses the right. What we do say is that the influence of the early years is strong and lasting and will help determine behavior throughout life.

A World of Feeling Not Reason

While it is true the small child is conscious of the acts and reactions of persons near him and gets from them his cues about himself and develops his response, the world of the young child is one of feeling. Though he has not yet entered the world of thought, of analysis, and of reasoning about himself and about those around him, he does have a well-developed sense of feeling. The physical touch, the emotional climate, the tone of voice, as well as the atmosphere of the family in general, is felt very early.

A parent's voice is important in the development of the child. It is not always *what* is said to the child but rather *how* it is conveyed. A warmth of feeling is just as effectively conveyed through the parent's voice as it is through physical contact. This is why it can be said that the child is much more conscious of the tone of voice than of the words that are spoken. He is more aware of the way something is said than of what is being said.

In addition, the child is not helped during the early years when parents try to reason with him or expect him to learn right from wrong by experience. At this time the child is dependent on parents for direction. He is not able to rationalize and to think clearly through the implications of his actions whether good or bad. He is dependent on his parents to settle on definite rules and in so doing guide him in the development of a moral sense. It is better to let the child know what is expected and that obedience and disobedience carry consequences.

Phyllis McGinley in her book *Sixpence in Her Shoe* describes the need of small children:

Their peace of mind, their safety, rests on grown-up authority; and it is that childish reliance which invalidates the worth of reasoning too much with them. The longer I lived in a house with children, the less importance I put on cooperatively threshing out matters of conduct or explaining to them our theories of discipline. If I had to do it over again I wouldn't reason with them at all until they arrived at an *age* of reason. . . . I would give them rules to follow. I would try to be just, and I would try even harder to be strict. I would do no arguing. Children, in their hearts, like laws. Authority implies an ordered world, which is what they—and, in the long run, most of the human race—yearn to inhabit. In law there is freedom. Be too permissive and they feel lost and alone. Children are forced to live very rapidly in order to live at all. They are given only a few years in which to learn hundreds of thousands of things about life and the planet and themselves. They haven't time to spend analyzing the logic behind each command or taboo, and they resent being pulled away by it from their proper business of discovery.[2]

This is in keeping with authorities who tell us that the small child becomes confused if made to reason and decide his own conduct. It takes away his childhood, his freedom, and his happiness. In preadolescence and adolescence, the young person wants to know reasons behind restrictions and rules, and parents should take the time to share the rationale behind them. But the small child becomes bogged down with such details if they are given to him before he is able to think in these terms and before he can cope with the implications. The young child needs rules, and when the parent is too permissive or when the child needs to make decisions of conduct, he becomes frustrated and fearful.

Paul Tournier writes in his small book, *To Resist or to Surrender?* that

there are many parents who do not want to argue with their children for every mistake. They reserve their authority for serious matters. But then it is too late. By forever giving in they lose all authority. Alexis Carrel has pointed out that most parents give in to their children's whims when they are small, the very age when they need a firm hand. The parents laugh at their children's antics then, and later in adolescence try to lay down the law, the very time when children need more freedom in order to gain their own experience.[3]

If parents exercise proper control in the early years, they can relax later because the child will have developed controls. But if the limits and controls are lacking in the early years, the child will be at a loss in later years and will likely react and rebel against any kind of control.

Because the young child is eager to win approval and love, he responds to the will of adults, particularly parents from whom he senses love and good will. Parents who demand certain clear things of the young child will find a child who will start to demand the best of himself. "Our chief want," wrote Emerson, "is someone who will make us do what we can." This is particularly true of this early age. So the child is dependent on the parents, not only for food and clothing, but for knowing right from wrong.

Clear and Consistent

What parents expect should be clear and consistent. Expectations ought to be consistent because the child becomes confused if what is allowed one day is not allowed the next or if the parents do what the child is corrected for. Children become confused if parents are not clear. Confused parents raise confused children.

Parents' own behavior plays an important part. If a parent strikes the child in anger, the child will be prompted to do likewise, no matter how nicely the parent may rationalize and attempt to train otherwise. The philosophy of don't do as I do but do as I say has very little appeal to the child. In the field of anger and hostility, as well as love, patience, and kindness, the child will be what the parent is.

Direct orders are best during the early years. Let the noes be few but consistent, and in love. During these years, for the child's physical and emotional well-being, parents should require obedience.

Parents need to decide on limits, seek to be consistent in what the limits are, and enforce them. Limits can be standards for the child to meet, a kind of challenge, if set in the right spirit. When anything goes, the child is uncomfortable, ill at ease, and insecure. To feel good a child needs a sense of coming up to expectations. And there are few, if any, things more satisfying to a child than the feeling that he is living up to his parents' expectations, that he is growing up.

James L. Hymes, Jr., writes:

You must draw the line at what you will take from your child. Have standards. Just be reasonable in what you expect. Adjust your demands to what a youngster your child's age can reasonably do. Set limits but when you stop undesirable behavior, don't tear down the child. Stop the act but keep the child feeling good about himself. And be generous in your praise when your youngster does come through. Nothing builds for better feelings than when you can honestly say, "That was a good job. You're really growing up."[4]

Because parents love, they consistently set limits on the child's acts. But limits should always convey authority and not insult. Dr. David R. Mace puts it strongly. "The idea that loving a child is letting him do what he likes is a pernicious falsehood! . . . Just as you hold him until he can walk by himself, and tie his laces till he can tie them himself, so you control his actions till he can control them himself."

A congressional report concerning juvenile delinquency states that in looking at punishment in the context of the emotional relationship between parent and child, the critical point seems to be whether the disciplinary measures are consistent or not, whether they are cruel or firm and kindly, whether they are given with calmness or anger, and most important, whether they are given by a parent who really loves the child, not one who is indifferent or hostile to the youngster.

A child, during these early years, needs to learn that his acts have consequences. This is another reason that commands and rules should be clear, and punishment or reward should be consistent.

Dr. Dale B. Harris compared two groups of adults who had gone through nursery school in the 1920s. One group came from homes with strict standards, where the child's schooling, contacts, and experiences were closely supervised by the parents. The second group came from homes where the child had much more liberty to do as he pleased. The study found that adults from the disciplined group were much more self-assured and more satisfied with their jobs and family life. They also had happier memories of their childhood.

Most emotional problems, according to Dr. Peter Crowford, a child psychologist of Augusta, Georgia, came not as a result of firm discipline but lack of firm discipline. A child's first virtue is obedience. When a distinguished French officer asked George Washington's mother how she managed to rear such a splendid son, she replied, "I taught him to obey."

As I wrote in the book *Seven Things Children Need:*

At times discipline may hurt, physically and emotionally, but the parent does his child an injustice to hold off discipline because it may hurt momentarily. If a child breaks an arm, setting the bone will be painful. The child may beg the parent to prevent having it set. Does a parent consider letting the child risk being crippled to avoid the pain of the moment? . . . Why risk making the child a moral cripple by refusing to provide the positive training which produces good character?"[5]

Positive and Persistent

Parents accomplish much more through positive guidance than with negative statements. Threats, name calling, insults, warnings, accusations, shaming, and competitive techniques lead the child to feel bad about himself and lead to wrong behavior. Saying no too often, and don't touch and stop it, soon becomes nagging dialogues. Though it is true the child needs fences, he is frustrated if everywhere he turns there are fences.

Constant criticism conveys to the child the idea that he does not belong, nor is he wanted or liked. Criticism is seldom a solution and severs ties of closeness.

All behavior is caused. There are reasons why the child responds the way he does, so the parent must look for the causes of unacceptable behavior. When parents are on edge, irritated, or emotionally upset, it will affect the child's behavior. When a parent is happy, relaxed, and loving, the child absorbs these feelings also.

Thoughtfulness for others has a great deal to do with developing proper conduct, so the parent teaches the child to respect others and to care for others by the example the parent sets in talk and action.

Sometimes parents invite misbehavior and wrong response by asking for a negative response. To ask, "Are you ready for bed?" invites a no. But to say, "It's time for bed. Take your doll with you," makes it easy. To say, "You should not use a hammer here, but I'll get you a board" is positive and calls forth a positive response. A child who is told he is careless, messy, lazy, rude, or a little devil will come to think of himself in this way and will be just what parents tell him he is. On the other hand, if parents concentrate on the positive and find good things, praise the child for being considerate, courteous, and well behaved, the child will seek to live up to these traits. Good conduct is built on success experiences rather than on negative statements.

Marilyn Bonham writes:

Much of the secret to your own success in making your requests understood and complied with is the manner in which you ask your child to obey your direction. Friendliness with firmness is usually the prudent combination. Threats rarely work, and only bring forth further cascades of "no." Offer threats and alternatives only when you really mean them and can follow through. Remember that your child will pay more attention to five reasonable rules than to fifteen unessential ones! Such is the simple mathematics of the three-year-old![6]

Especially with the young child, parents ought to avoid using good and bad labels. Parents can be firm in curbing the child's impulses without labeling his character or belittling him for wrong behavior. If the parent consistently calls the child bad, the child will accept this as the parent's evaluation. And this attitude undermines the development of needed self-respect.

The child learns right from wrong, not only by clear commands and rules, but also by exposure to the moral behavior of others. First, the consistent demands of parents and the example of parents are important. Also the telling and reading of stories about real people dramatize values in a way the small child enjoys and understands. Someone suggested a family should share something each day from its own history, something about childhood, parents, grandparents, and others. Such stories are of great interest to the child and tell what is valued in the parents' own experience.

Finally the sense of responsibility must grow from within. Says Kathryn Aschliman, in *The Family in Today's Society*, responsibility "is fed and directed by values absorbed in the home. Parents want children's response to spring from ultimate values, among which are reverence for life and concern for human welfare. This influences the amount of TV watching done in the home. An increasing number of parents are not willing to let murderers and thugs influence their children in their own living room. Toys, too, that allow children to rehearse the positive activities of life are thoughtfully purchased."[7]

Mother Needed

At no time in the life of the child is mother more important than during the early years. At no time is the mother's own purpose, persuasion, personhood, and power more significant. Her goals, strong sense of direction, emotional stability, intellectual pursuits, along with such characteristics as strictness with love, persistence, consistency, clear expectations, and confidence will have much to do with the child's development. At no time will the presence or absence of such traits exert a more fundamental influence. It is not a new observation to note that children who are able to stand for themselves and move with security and confidence usually come from families where the mother was strong in the above characteristics and in her sense of direction.

What parents, and particularly the mother who is so close to the heart of the child, expect from the child becomes the child's moral compass. It is during these early years that a large part of obedience is learned, and the pattern is set. Since the mother is usually closest to the child during these years, she has a great influence on his behavior.

Of course, the father is important also, particularly as he stands strong beside his wife with love and warm emotional support to mother and child. At no time are the words, popularized by Charlie Shedd, more true, "The best thing a father can do for his children is to love their mother." That love must be seen in kindly acts and felt in the atmosphere.

Very early the child senses whether or not mother and father are together in what is expected. One of the causes for mixed-up children and emotional wrecks in youth is parents who are at odds in their approach to training and discipline, for the child has learned to pit parents against each other. It is surprising how early the small child senses this kind of disagreement.

A summary of a disheartening poll conducted recently by one of our popular magazines says that parents seem to be retreating on all fronts, confused, often panicky, and afraid of their children. They are afraid to set guidelines and limits and to establish dos and don'ts even though they know they should.

This poll, a survey of 660 women from all parts of the country, revealed that these parents know they are ruining their children's lives by being too permissive, yet confessed they felt helpless. One-half of the mothers admitted they tailored their lives to their children's likes and dislikes. They do not discuss today's moral issues with their children. The result is children who are at a loss to find their way. They also lose respect for parents who will not give the guidance they need and basically want so badly.

Thus, a primary responsibility of parents is to work early, seriously, and continually at their own system of values. Life is ever changing; old standards, often clear and simple, become inadequate guides in today's complicated life. And if parents are growing morally themselves, they must constantly reevaluate their own standards to see if they are clear moral ones. This means that the values by which parents live must be more than goals of behavior to lift up before their children. They must be principles that parents themselves practice.

As Christians, our understanding of values does not begin with ourselves. It begins with God, the source of truth, beauty, and good. As we ourselves respond in love, faith, and obedience, we come to understand God's will for us. Our principles must be in the atmosphere of the home, as it were, in the very air we breathe.

Let It Be in Love

The young child's survival and well-being depend just as much on the parents' love and closeness as on proper formula, food, and shelter. Victor Hugo wrote, "The supreme happiness in life is the conviction that we are loved." And Rabindranath Tagore said, "He only may chastise who loves." Love is the best form of guidance.

Discipline, guidance, and control go wrong unless they exist in the framework of good feeling, affection, and love. The actual methods of control are never as important as the parents' consistency and ever-present spirit of wanting to help in love. The child must feel the good will of the parent, not that the child will always love the parent for everything he says or does, but the child must sense that the parent has his best interests at heart. The child grows when praise, kind words, and encouragement are given. One mother put drawings and schoolwork in her husband's lunch box, so that when he returned home in the evening he came with praise and compliments for the children. Physical demonstrations of love, good fun, smiling faces, and a good sense of humor always help, but the child wants more than sympathetic playmates. The child wants guidance, and the child becomes confused if parents allow what they know is wrong.

All of this was put into a positive statement by an unknown parent:

Children have the right to be immature and opportunistic, to have "accidents," and to be permitted to grow gradually into compliance with grown-up standards. Our children need from us the opportunity for experiences within their capacity to deal, our assurance that we are there to help them when they need it, our encouragement in their attempts to accomplish, our acceptance of their efforts without belittling, our recognition of their successes, and our readiness to stop them when they need to be stopped.

Discussion Statement and Questions

1. Discuss the statement by Tryon Edwards preceding this chapter, page 26.
2. Discuss why parents should demand obedience from the young child rather than trying to reason with him.

3. Do you agree that the young child is not helped when parents try to reason with him or expect him to learn from experience?
4. Discuss the element of consistency in punishment.
5. It is rather common and easy to use labels. All of us have heard parents call their child "a little devil" or similar names and also observed that the child will seek to live up to the name given him. Discuss the impact of labels on the child's behavior.
6. Discuss a child's first virtue, obedience.
7. How do you see the place of baby-sitters during this early period when the child needs to be close to parents and needs to learn obedience?

Whether it be for good or evil, the education of the child is principally derived from its own observation of the actions, words, voice, and looks of those with whom it lives.—John Webb

Since for better or worse human nature is contagious, the children are pretty apt to catch it. That can be fine or awful and at one time or another it is likely to be both. When it's fine, any parent beams. There's no better confirmation of inherent virtue. When it's bad, any parent finds it rough. Who wants to look at a certified copy of his own faults?—Leontine Young

Children have more need of models than of critics. —Joseph Joubert

The child usually becomes what he is trained to sacrifice for, to love, admire and worship.—Ray F. Koonce

Fenelon wrote many years ago: Beware of fatiguing them [your children] with ill-judged exactness. If virtue offers itself to the child under a melancholy and constrained aspect, while liberty and license present themselves under an agreeable form, all is lost, and your labor is in vain.

The child is father of the man.—Wordsworth

Age of Imitation—
Age Eight to Age Twelve

There was a child went forth each day. And the first object he looked upon that object he became.—Walt Whitman

A cartoonist pictures a puzzled father with his elbows on the dinner table. He is looking down the length of the table at his wife and complaining, "Why can't they know that it is wrong for everybody but me to sit this way?"

As the child moves into the period of preadolescence, what is sometimes called the middle childhood years, he enters a time where he imitates the adults around him. This is the time when the example of the parents becomes exceedingly important. Many years ago John Balguy wrote, "Whatever parent gives his children good instructions and sets them at the same time a bad example, may be considered as bringing them food in one hand and poison in the other."

With, of course, variations among children, the first seven years are ones when the child is dependent on parents for guidance, rules, and the setting of standards. Although these continue to be important for the eight- to twelve-year-olds, the example of the parent is now a primary factor in the child's developing concepts of right and wrong.

Characterististics of the Preadolescent

While it is not the purpose of this section to discuss all the unique characteristics of the preadolescent, it will be helpful to understand some of these as parents seek to guide the child in the development of a moral conscience and acceptable behavior.

A healthy young preadolescent is an active, noisy youngster who finds it hard to sit still. He will practice endlessly at developing skills in sports, music, and other areas that catch his fancy. This is good and should be encouraged, since it develops self-confidence. Where he is affirmed, he will develop great interest and be diligent, preparing for the times in adolescence when he will be driven to have feelings of inadequacy about himself.

Sometimes this period is spoken of as the "smart" age. The child likes to share what he knows, picks up quickly every accurate statement, reacts against injustice, and is very exacting of himself and others. One writer says that the preadolescent child has the memory of an elephant for the things that strike his interest. Make him a promise to take him fishing or to a ball game, and he will never forget it.

Sometimes it seems a child in this age loses all respect for manners. He is noisy and intellectually curious. He has a great desire to do things, to be useful, and to assume responsibility. He shuns baby ways and yearns to be needed like an adult. The parent who can steer this interest into the right areas does well.

At this age there is a great urge to belong to a group, club, or gang of his peers. The child needs a small group of intimate friends. Girls want to be with girls and boys with boys, and it is upsetting to be exiled from a group. It is almost a sin to be different in any way, particularly in clothes, manners, and interests. This means a good gang or group is of tremendous help in shaping attitudes toward life and toward others.

Home to the preadolescent is a necessary and natural base from which to operate, but it is more "a place you go when you can't go anywhere else." The child likes to go elsewhere, yet needs the security of a happy home.

This is also the time when the child becomes more inquisitive about sex and human relationships. The forbidden sex words are shared.

What the child needs during these years is to have a climate in which to express ideas freely. He needs to air his thoughts and feelings and will benefit greatly if parents use this time to know him better and to understand him. The preadolescent is quite capable of reasoning if the right kind of atmosphere prevails. During these few years a great deal of consolidation and maturing takes place. The clay is not hard as yet, and the parents have, during these years, a chance to play a special role in shaping the child's thinking. It is a good time to participate in all kinds of activities with the child. He will join freely now in things he may refuse to do later. It is also a good time to help him develop skills that interest him and to explore wider horizons. His basic need is to accomplish to the point where he believes in himself and has a sense of measuring up in the estimation of the gang, and particularly in the estimation of his parents.

Development of Conscience

Perhaps the most important developmental task during this period of later childhood is the acquiring of a conscience. Here are the possibilities for a rapidly developing conscience. Conscience is the ability to distinguish right from wrong. This ability is learned according to the moral standards of home, church, community, and other influences, but particularly through the home. Conscience implies that the child is developing internalized control for right or wrong behavior.

A person is not born with a conscience. The conscience is trained, taught, and begins to function in early childhood. Of course, it continues to develop and change all through life as it continues to be guided. The responsibility for the content of the conscience rests primarily on parents, although the other agencies mentioned set moral standards also.

All persons develop some kind of conscience by what is taught and caught from surroundings. We see, therefore, why some have a conscience about some things while others do not. It depends on the instruction.

To have a strong conscience means to have such a clear idea of what is right or wrong that it controls behavior. Studies show that children with a strong conscience come from families where there are warm, loving, and caring parents. On the other hand, parents who tend to be cold and aloof as well as overly demanding and meticulous may cause their children to be weak in confronting temptations when left on their own.

When the home is warm and loving, and the parents, though considered strict, exercise a loving response when the child disobeys, the child will seek to measure up to what the parents desire and will be quick to confess wrong. The child prizes the love of the parents. However, when the home is cold and indifferent and the response to wrongdoing does not clearly express love for the child's welfare, the child will be fearful and slow in confessing wrong and will learn to lie in order to protect himself.

Strength of conscience often depends more on the identification the child makes with parents, church, school, and community ideals and standards than on a lot of instruction. Here again the child is a great imitator and learns chiefly from example. Where does the child identify? This identity creates the roots of the child's superego (conscience) and builds his sense of right and wrong. Since, for example, the boy cannot take his father's place, he can at least seek to be like him, eventually hoping to marry a woman similar to the one his father chose.

This identification is fashioned by what his parents are and what they expect of him rather than his personal understanding of all the implications of what is right and wrong. The development of conscience, one might say, is almost automatic because it emerges before a great deal of the child's own independent judgment does. This identification with adults helps give him an anchor and strengthens his becoming a civilized human being with personal control. The child who does not identify with his parents will develop a weak conscience, with weak controls over his own behavior, and may join the other juvenile delinquents in society.

Dr. Ralph Heynen in his book, *The Secret of Christian Family Living,* says, "The driving forces of life are emotional, rather than intellectual. Man is a thinking and rational being, but we are not as rational as we think we are. . . . A person grows up to be truthful, honest, and generous, not because he is intellectually convinced that such virtues are best for him, but because he has seen these virtues in practices and precepts in his home and cultural setting."[1]

An article in *Parents' Magazine* points out that during this stage the child develops the basic disposition that will influence him later in life when he decides who his friends will be, what vocation he will choose, what life-style he will have, what kind of relationships he will develop with other people, and what set of values he will establish.

This also is the time the child establishes touchstones of belief and values, so he will have something to hang on to during the storms of temptation and uncertainty that come in adolescence.

Power of Example

All this leads again to the fact that the child in a most important way during the preadolescent period mirrors what he sees going on in his home. What a parent says has little effect unless it reflects what a parent does and is. So a parent dare not be or do what he does not want his child to be or do. The child begins life without knowing what is expected. He watches others and tries to do what they do. All parents have, at times, been amused at the way their children imitate those around them, but it is more than amusing. It becomes a way of life.

Ella May Miller, long-time speaker on a radio program dealing with family issues, told of a young fellow who, as a Boy Scout treasurer, juggled figures to enable him to buy candy for some of his friends. After listening to his father's outburst when he learned of the incident, Jack asked very seriously, "Why, Dad, that was only five dollars. The other night I heard you laugh when you told how you cheated the government out of five hundred dollars income tax!"

Miller commented, "The parent who laughs at speed limits, who 'gets by' as much as possible in his civic and church obligations can expect no more from his children.

Yes, what we do as parents speaks louder than what we say! Our day by day examples and family conversations help our children form standards of their own."[2]

In myriad ways the child imitates his parents. Charles, as a young boy, walked pensively with his hands clasped behind his back just as his father did. Imitation is the sincerest form of flattery. It is also the most effective form of learning, especially at this time of life.

Dr. William E. Davis in an article, "Children Need Models to Follow, Not Orders," says that if we considered the amount of time and effort devoted to advising and giving orders to our children, we would be amazed at how little influence we exert on the kind of people our children will become by telling them what to do.

But we can have a profound influence through providing them with a clearly perceived and attractive model to imitate. This involves being persons with adult integrity, and our striving for self-development should take priority over self-conscious efforts to mold our children.

Alice V. Keliher writes:

Young children have built-in stethoscopes with which they assess the feelings that surround them. They note well the attitudes and the behavior of their parents and of the other important adults in their lives. They file away these notes, often in deep unconscious storehouses, to guide their responses not only to today's human encounters but also to tomorrow's. Watch them at their house-keeping and doll play, or in their improvised dramatics, for clues of what they have learned from the people around them.

Standards of behavior and courtesy, expressions of respect, demonstration of generosity of spirit, of neighborliness, of decency—these are filed away for further reference. Note the families that generation after generation provide public spirited citizens. These attitudes do not come by way of the genes and chromosomes. They come by example.[3]

Also respect for others is developed at home. These attitudes are developed by observing how parents speak to the salesperson who comes to the house, how they speak to the clerk at the store, or how they speak over the telephone or with a neighbor. Attitudes toward people and concerns are reflected in family discussions about others and about the needs of the community and the world.

In these growing-up years from eight to twelve, reading is at an all-time high. The right kind of books and magazines in the home will help determine values.

Reading stories to the child, long after the child has learned to read by himself, is another important way of talking things over and developing feelings of togetherness from which the sharing of confidences and concerns arise. Stories of good conduct, bravery in doing right, honesty in different and difficult situations should be read, particularly in preadolescence, when the child wants to imitate what seems to be heroic and challenging. A child learns to feel compassion and love for others through such reading. And this needs to take precedence over dirty dishes and other tasks of Mother and Father.

Children seek to follow those they love and admire. The kind of person a child becomes depends on the kinds of adults he admires. The sense of right and wrong seems really to depend on the emotional ties which exist between the child and his parents. Careful, scientific studies show that nondelinquents have a satisfying relationship with their parents in early life which delinquents do not. The importance of the right example is what the writer of Proverbs 29:15b had in mind. "A child left to himself brings shame to his mother." The biblical picture is of an animal left to stray in the pasture. Left without careful training, it achieves no usefulness.

Because a child will imitate those he admires, it is

important that parents be proper persons. Also the implications of television and the impact of heroes and persons on the child cannot be overemphasized. It is no accident that one of the large church denominations found, in a study several years ago, that more than one-half of those who entered the Christian ministry had decided on this vocation by the age of eleven.

A counselor working with boys at a correctional center had them reflect on the kind of homes they came from and write down a code for parents, using as a basis things in which they thought their parents failed. This is part of the code: "Don't get strung out from too much booze or too many pills. When we see our parents reaching for these crutches we get the idea that nobody goes out there alone, that it's perfectly O.K. to go for a bottle or a capsule when things get too heavy. Remember, your children are great imitators. We lose respect for parents who tell us to behave one way while they are behaving another way."

As the child moves into preadolescence, rules remain important to him. Witness what the child says in his play. He will refer to the rules of the game. He does not like to play any longer with younger boys and girls because they do not keep the rules.

It is also a time when the child will bargain about keeping the rules. One mother made a bargain with her ten-year-old. "I don't want to be a scolding mother," she said, "so this week I am getting a handful of pennies. We'll divide the pennies. Any time one of you hears me scolding, ask me for a penny. But if I find you misbehaving, you must give me a penny. Is it a deal?" Children in the middle-age group love such a challenge.

Psychiatrists and family counselors now point out that the worst thing we can do to our children is to be too soft. Children whose parents say they love them too much to punish them are like cars driving down a street without traffic signs. Confused, bewildered, these youngsters may provoke their parents with worse and worse behavior in trying to get across the message, "If we go far enough wrong, maybe someone will care enough to stop us."

Youngsters themselves ask for stricter discipline. Some years ago the Kansas Council for Children and Youth interviewed high school students about their relationships with their parents. Nearly one-third felt their parents were not strict enough. Several commented that they were confused by the failure of their parents to agree on discipline. "I do a lot of baby-sitting," one girl wrote on her questionnaire, "and I am surprised how many parents allow their small children to make everyone in the house miserable. It's hard for me to believe that a child who is allowed to throw tantrums in order to get her way is going to be more lovable fifteen years from now."

If the atmosphere has been one of love and consistency, the eight- to twelve-year-old has a conscience that begins to express itself. If obedience was demanded and realized during the earlier years, the conscience will be developing, particularly in these years.

The same delinquent mentioned above said concerning rules: "If you catch us lying, stealing or being cruel, get tough. Let us know why what we did was wrong. Impress on us the importance of not repeating such behavior. When we need punishment, dish it out. But let us know you still love us, even though we have let you down. It'll make us think twice before we make the same move again."

Dr. Sheldon Glueck suggests that "unless you build up within the person a stronger motivation for behaving himself than fear, as soon as the officer or father is away, the child will twiddle his thumb at him and go and sin some more." Stronger motivations for right behavior must be built into the character of the child; this is done through a right example set before the child and through the steadfast love shown toward him. In a survey of ten thousand delinquents it was found they had one thing in common—a lack of affection shown toward them. A child who receives warm affection responds with love and obedience. Urban Steinmetz comments, "I am beginning to believe that a parent can't make too many mistakes if love continues to come through."

A consistent love is what the Senate Subcommittee on Juvenile Delinquency emphasized in pointing out that a child needs to know that he can always count on his parents. The report says that the lines of character and self-control are erected in the individual, if at all, by definite rules administered fairly and firmly. This is done through love and praise for right and through withdrawal of approval (not love) for violations. Where there is only approval or neglect, there is no dynamic force through which the child can create or identify himself with standards of behavior and the life and conduct of his parents.

Clara Lambert writes, "Your children want rules, laws, and regulations, but they like the 'rubber band' type which can be stretched a little but not broken. You cannot afford to be spineless or afraid of your children. You must know how to compromise graciously, be firm without rancor, be fair, and even look the other way sometimes to sidestep an unimportant issue."[4]

The Goal

Of course, the ultimate purpose of training is to help the child become an independent, thinking person who will be able to face life and decide moral issues. An encouraging word is extremely important when the child does choose the good. By a word of criticism or comfort, the child's spirit can be stifled or strengthened. Many parents are guilty of injustice against their children by offering only correction and rebuke. Conversely, when the child feels enveloped in love and warmed with trust, he is in optimum circumstances for making right choices. The home is the place to help children develop these inner responses and strengths so that they can learn to fly.

When parents in the home are realistic about their own mistakes, they help their children be realistic in evaluating themselves. As parents we may correct or punish our children too severely or cut them off with an impatient answer. Children may recover from the hurt more quickly than we recover from the feelings of guilt over what we have done.

Gibson Winters suggests that parents can build a whole new dimension of life for their children by confessing their injustices and asking for forgiveness. Such experiences help children see that forgiveness is part of the very fabric of human relationships. In addition, children learn that the parents are under a higher law of righteousness and that they are human and not God. They learn that a transgression does not end the relationship. They learn that the transgressions can be opportunities for deeper personal relationships.

Discussion Statements and Questions

1. What other characteristics of the preadolescent can you name?
2. Discuss the development of the conscience.
3. Can you think of times and ways your child imitated you in something?

4. Discuss the idea that a parent should first give thought to self-improvement rather than trying to mold the character of the child.
5. Are there exceptions to the "like-parent-like-child" idea?
6. Do you feel that the eight- to twelve-year-olds like to play and live by the rules?
7. Discuss the last part of this chapter regarding love coming through under all circumstances.
8. What does the statement "A child becomes like those he admires" have to say regarding movie and television characters? His companions during this age as well as his parents?

It is the plan of God that the authority of parents over their children be exercised in an atmosphere of manifest love. The word "manifest" is important. It means a love that the children can recognize at all times, even when they are punished. It is a love that expresses itself in hundreds of little ways, all centering around the deep interest of the parents in the work, the play, the prayers, the total welfare of their children. It is the basis on which the children build up an unshakable confidence in their parents.—Joseph T. McGroin and John L. Thomas Liguorian

Let the young person know that it's all right to think differently from his parents and other adults.

Help him to realize that an idea is not necessarily good because it is modern, or poor simply because it is old-fashioned. An idea is good if it is appropriate and effective, regardless of the era in which it was popular.

Help him examine the reasons for his beliefs. It is not enough for a boy or girl to believe or disbelieve something only because his parents do. A belief should make sense to the person who holds it.—Margaret Hill

The teen years are those in which the parents should be listening, praying, available, and loving—especially loving. The teen-ager needs his parents and down deep wants them.

Age of Inspiration—
Age Thirteen to Adulthood

A common comment by parents of teen-agers to those who have younger children is, "You think you've got problems now. Just wait until they hit the teens."

Adolescence means to grow. It means to grow from childhood into maturity. While the young child is most conscious of what he is told and the eight- to twelve-year-old is concerned about who tells him, the adolescent is more concerned about why? The teen-ager is in search of meanings, experiences, and discussions. This is the age to inspire by great ideas and principles. In addition, adolescents need heroes. If heroes are not offered them, they will create their own as they have done with their current idols.

At the age of thirteen the adolescent knows pretty well what parents believe and practice and what parents will likely do under different circumstances. Now the questions

Why should I? and Why shouldn't I? test the parents' own identity and reasoning. This is one of the major reasons why adolescence is so difficult for parents and teens.

Traits of the Teens

While it is easier to label the adolescent than to seek to understand him, and it is always dangerous to generalize because of great differences among youth, certain characteristics become clear in the great amount of study devoted to adolescence.

In a poll adults, parents, clergy, and others were asked: "What do you think are the most urgent areas of concern for teen-agers?" and "What are the areas of greatest inner conflict faced by most adolescents?" The answers were: rebellion, generation gap, dating, family stress, and drugs. But when the teen-agers were asked the same questions, answering anonymously, they said their most urgent areas of concern and inner conflict had to do with faith, unresolved guilt, vocation, acceptance by adults and peers, personal identity, and approval from the entire adult world. A few wrestled at times over their own fears of being different, emotionally and even mentally. It was evident that the teen-agers were running frightened and insecure.

Adolescence is a time of doubt, uncertainty, and awkwardness that is accentuated by the search to find one's own selfhood. An adolescent wants the privilege and responsibilities of an adult, yet feels uncertain about how ready he is.

The adolescent needs to adjust to rapid physical changes. These are dramatic, with boys increasing in strength by 50 percent during teen years. Girls become women in appearance and in their ability to bear children. There are also great social adjustments in learning to get along with others. This is terribly important and disturbing.

Parents have a lot of concern during the teen years. The teen has a lot of concerns also. Boy-girl problems become real. He is searching for his own identity. Serious thoughts about plans for making a living and about vocational choices are necessary. He has mixed-up feelings about emotional changes. Decisions of right and wrong and the establishment of one's own values can be confusing. Whereas answers regarding religious outlook were given to him in the past, now the adolescent is driven by peers and different situations to decide for himself.

If there is one thing that studies have shown, it is that adolescents have very similar problems and concerns. Paul H. Landis, author of numerous books about and for young people, has collected more than one thousand autobiographies of students during later teens and has traced personality development through these years. One of the most prominent things is the description of feelings and fears of teen years. He lists problems most often mentioned in order of priority.

1. Inferiority feelings. Teens do not feel capable of meeting life. Many try to compensate for such feelings by overdoing clothes, dressing to draw attention, becoming show-offs, being class bullies, withdrawing, becoming critical of themselves and others, or developing feelings of jealousy and envy.

The truth is that each person is inferior to other persons in some things, and each person also excels in certain things. Everyone has something to contribute.

The great drive for superiority today causes feelings of inferiority. Martha Weinman Lear points out that middle-class parents vigorously compete with one another in raising the best-educated, the best-dressed, the best-fed, the best-mannered, the best-cultured, the best-medicated, and the best-adjusted child on the block. An ordinary, common, average child is a hard thing for many American parents to accept, even Christian ones.[1]

2. Daydreaming. This is a problem particularly for girls. It is a way of escaping inferiority feelings, because in fantasy they become the central character. Fantasy builds a world more attractive than the one in which they actually live. Boys dream more of things outside themselves.

3. Sex problems. For boys it is how to control their desires. For girls it is how to behave on a date, going too far, and how much physical contact.

4. Temperament. Moodiness and bad disposition worry teens. They get anxious about meeting people and about manners. One day the adolescent may feel love for everyone and the next day feel hate for the world. He may want to save all society one day, and the next he may feel like rebelling against it all. One day he may feel selfish, and the next he may feel very unselfish. Sometimes he feels very close to God, at other times he feels very distant from him. Sometimes he may feel deep love for his parents, and at other times he may feel deep hate. But moods are a part of growing up. It is more important to pay attention to the models they admire than to their moods.

5. Religion. During the teen years the adolescent is challenged with social concern. He begins to want to *do* something to improve the world. He debates questions about God, heaven, hell, immortality, and the reason for living. All questions and doubts demand quick answers. Parents are challenged about their own values and standards.

6. Independence from parents. Here the frequent phrase of a girl to her mother is "Oh, you wouldn't understand." And the fellow is certain that Dad is an "old fogy" who has lost all touch with things. At times teens become almost

totally disillusioned with parents and adults and chafe at adult demands. Opinions of peers are often valued higher than those of parents or teachers. Yet surveys still indicate that youth value their parents' viewpoints above any other.

Adolescence is a period of inconsistency. The young person may at times be pleasure-crazy and at other times pleasure-denying. He may feel totally uninhibited in one area and totally repressed in another. He may indulge in excesses, even in alcohol and drugs, yet be a vegetarian and maintain a strict diet. He may speak with enormous idealism, altruism, and self-sacrifice; yet be very egocentric, selfish, rude, and thoughtless. He may follow a strict code of ethics in one area and be critical of parents and others whom he will hold to the line, yet lie and cheat himself in other areas. As someone has pointed out, the only consistency is inconsistency, and the only prediction is the unpredictability in the life of the adolescent.

A lot of study has been given to the big areas of disagreement between teen-agers and parents. The striking thing is that they have changed so little from generation to generation. Some of these areas are:

1. Spending money
2. Outside activities and social life, such as dating and what time to be in at night
3. Sharing work at home and feeling unloved in being made responsible
4. Doing schoolwork conscientiously
5. What clothes to wear
6. The family car, particularly for boys

It is good to realize that although Mother and Dad lived in a different day they had about the same struggles as youth have now.

Testing, Testing, Testing

When a child's moral awareness begins, he may not be rebelling so much as testing. The adolescent is very "other" conscious in the sense that he is more aware of others outside the family and how they live. While the young child accepts authority, particularly as parents exercise it, and the eight- to twelve-year-old sees rules as something people, particularly his parents, obey; the adolescent is interested in the reason for certain behavior. He is now capable of understanding principles, and he quickly discerns injustice, hypocrisy, and dishonesty. He questions what he has accepted, and now knows he must decide what he will accept or reject for himself. While before he was a satellite of his parents, now he needs to be separated from them.

This always, to one degree or another, strains the relationship with adults and particularly the parents. What must be kept in mind is that such questioning and reaction is not so much a sign of rebellion as it is evidence of the child's moral awareness. Now he chooses to disobey or obey more on the basis of whether he sees a principle embodied in the action. To find out, he continually tests his ideas and actions against parents and others. By so doing he also tests whether they really believe what they say.

Dr. James Dobson in his book, *Hide or Seek,* says concerning the adolescent:

Let your manner convey your acceptance of him as an individual, even aiming your conversation a year or two above his head. Does this mean you have to pussyfoot with him when he has defied your authority or overstepped reasonable boundaries? Certainly not. It is possible to treat a child respectfully, even when punishment is necessary. In fact, during my years as a schoolteacher—at times seeing 225 teenagers in my classroom each day—I learned that youngsters will tolerate all sorts of rules and restrictions, provided you don't assault their ego. But if you make them feel childish and foolish, brace yourself for wrath and hostility.[2]

Rebellion against religious faith or rules of the family is often a means for the youth to assert individual integrity or independence from parents. To the extent that the individual remains psychologically unweaned, he tends to unconsciously identify the church and God with parents. He then tends to respond to authority or rules in a manner which befits his deepest feelings toward one or both parents.

Adolescence is a time when young people are eager to try their own wings, to break the apron strings, to develop and demonstrate growing maturity. Parents are driven by the fear that their child will make hurtful mistakes, and they seek to prevent such mistakes by taking a strong hand, often without adequate explanation. In these cases a clash is practically inevitable.

Parents have such a strong desire to see their children turn out well that they are often unaware that, instead of making decisions *with* their teen-agers, they are making the decisions *for* them.

Almost invariably, when parent and child have already passed through a lifetime of meaningful and reasonable rules and regulations, even the rebellious nature of the adolescent will not prevent him from striking a responsive chord. But for the parent who has only now begun to "clamp down" when adolescence encroaches on family happiness and serenity, trouble may well be ahead. "His capacity to think and the way he thinks will depend upon the equipment with which he began life, and the stimulus that has been given him through the books he has read, the situations in which he has been placed, and the people—parents, teachers, friends, and acquaintances—whom he has known."[3]

A Goal Is Important

Without a doubt much of the difficulty experienced today between teens and parents is because many teens have no goal toward which they are working. Because youth are required to be a certain age to hold a job, because of uncertainty about the future, or because parents are too preoccupied, youth have few plans beyond the present.

During this period a great deal of stability and character is gained if the teen-ager has certain goals in mind. The inspiration of a goal can work wonders.

Of course, there are short-range and long-range goals. For example, sports involve relatively short-range goals. The young person disciplines himself to be in shape for the team. He seeks to *excel* in a game or another kind of competition. A long-range goal can have tremendous influence, not only in stabilizing life, but also in learning discipline desired for life.

Here is an actual case of a family with two teen-age sons. The one, as he entered adolescence, looked forward to becoming a partner in his father's business. They talked about it. He geared his studies to this. He, to a great degree, disciplined himself in his choices of what to do or not to do by how it would contribute to his future. This prospect also determined his conduct to a surprising degree.

The second son seemed without goals, either short-range or long-range. Even in his last year of high school he had nothing definite in mind for his lifework. He had no project of any kind that held his interest. His life-style and conduct was a sharp contrast to his brother's. To him the gang was extremely important, and spending his evenings with the gang was all he looked forward to. His mother commented, "We didn't have near as much trouble with our older boy. He always seemed to have something to do."

A worthy and challenging goal can have a lot to do with choices and conduct during the tough and trying teens.

Peers and Parents

When the child becomes an adolescent, he appears to lose all respect for what parents say, and the word and conduct of his peers seem to take priority. Parents are tempted to divide the world of their son or daughter into the world of the family and the world of their child's friends. The importance of the peer group is an important element of development, and the parent needs to guard against driving the youth into the arms of his peers by cutting him off from warm home relationships.

Marilyn Bonham writes:

> But the normal adolescent needs both the warmth and security of his own home as well as the homogeneity of his group. Many parents make the mistake of forcing a choice. If they do they will place their children in terrible dilemmas, and create additional emotional hazards.
>
> To recognize that adolescent life requires these dual loyalties is the first step. The second step requires parents to treat their teenagers with the respect and sensitivity which is due any person who in six or eight years will be fully adult. Punishment of the teenager is just as necessary as punishment for the small child. But the manner in which it is carried out is of vital importance to the adolescent. So long as the relationship continues to run on a solid rock of respect and mutual trust, the occasional breakdowns that require discipline will not hurt. The worst accusation a teenager can hurl at his parents is that they are treating him like a child. The normal adolescent will not resent discipline, only the manner in which it is meted out.[4]

How an adolescent handles himself during this difficult period of relating to peers and parents is closely related to the kind of relationship the parents maintain. If the child feels that he is a person of worth at home and is accepted there on a mature level, he will handle the peer pressure. And parents can give their child a sense of importance by letting him be a part of family conferences and decisions, by asking his advice, and by sharing the activities, problems, responsibilities, and needs of the home. Although the peer group during the adolescent years appears to become a dominating influence and is important in meeting the needs of youth, one must also stress the stabilizing and supporting role of the home during this time of stretching, retreating, rejecting, and affirming.

As one parent said, "We owe it to our children to be unpopular with them sometimes when the pressure is on to follow the gang in something they should not do. They should be able to say, 'I'd be glad to go, but my parents are heels. They won't let me.' "

Setting Limits

Teen-agers need limits because of their intense drives. The limits should be set by the youth's degree of maturity, recognized in each person's capacity to accept responsibility.

Making moral decisions is one of the most difficult tasks that everyone faces. Grace and Fred M. Hechinger in their book *Teen-Age Tyranny* write, "It is an impossible [task] without the prerequisite of experience and knowledge, plus the prior mapping out of goals or conduct and targets of achievement."

In commenting on the necessity of rules the same authors say,

There is a vast difference between the age-old human tendency to try to get away with violation of rules, and the permissive removal of such rules and standards in the first place. The fact that laws are broken with great regularity, far from being an argument against the making of laws, is instead the most convincing reason why the laws are necessary. The "liberal" view that it is better to relax standards than to invite hypocrisy in the nonobservance of them overlooks the need of human beings for a frame of moral reference.

This is particulaly true of teenagers. No matter how strict the values, they will always test the limits to which they can go in circumventing them. The theory that by relaxing the rules youngsters will become more honest is a sentimental dream. It merely deprives them of the security of knowing right from wrong and makes it more difficult for them to decide how to behave and what to do or not do.[5]

Charles Frenkel of Columbia University said in the 1962 Conference of the Child Study Association that the lack of clear off-limits rules has deprived youth of an important privilege, to rebel.

Adolescents rebel by nature, but it often is a test of parental power as much as it is rebelling. The teen-ager wants to have a limit set on his actions.

In her article "Must Teens Be Tyrants?" LaVerna Klippenstein writes, "The adolescent's question to mother, 'Don't you trust me?' asked with the proper dash of teenage drama and hurt, needs often to be answered, 'I trust you on your own, but not when you think you must be a part of the crowd.' Properly chaperoned teen parties are no more an insult to young people than are traffic signals in an orderly town."[6]

Remember also that teen-agers expect authority to be expressed by their parents and that their unhappiness with a fair decision on the parents' part now does not mean that they will not be thankful later for the firmness. The important thing is that the manner or technique of the refusal can be wounding.

Methods of discipline need to vary, not only with different children, but with the same child at different age levels. A child under seven years of age should be required to obey for his own physical and emotional welfare. From this age, however, the parent should begin to lead the child to exercise self-control and personal responsibility. By the time a child is a teen-ager he must, if he is to be a disciplined adult, have learned to respect his parents, who through judgment, discernment, love, and experience have demonstrated their ability to help him.

A parent can discipline a four-year-old by spanking him, but a teen-ager needs counsel. For discipline to be effective, the method must be accommodated to the age and the individual needs of the child.

In one home a teen-ager was rebellious because he felt he did not get a sufficient allowance. The parents decided to speak with him about the details of the family budget. At the end of the discussion the boy turned to his father and said, "You've done a good job, Dad! I don't see how you managed to give us all so much."

While younger children cannot rationalize, they learn from repetition, from observing, and from firm guidance. But adolescence requires more explanation of why some things are right and why others are wrong or inappropriate.

Despite tension with parents studies show that 88.5 percent of teen-agers indicate that if they were parents of teen-agers they would be as strict with their children as their parents were with them, or more so.

One youth advisor said, "I'm glad that my parents held a close rein on me, for had I been permitted to do some things I wanted to do as a teen-ager, I would not be helping other youth today."

Studies of delinquents, who were known to hate people, church, school, laws, and their own age groups, disclosed strong evidence of their disliking themselves, whereas teen-agers who were developing more likable dispositions and personalities, not only liked themselves better, but also liked the people and institutions around them. Another revelation that was not surprising was that these latter teen-agers were better liked by the people around them.

James Dobson points out in *Hide or Seek* that it is the job of parents to provide a child with a healthy identity during the formative years in the home. This is done by teaching the child what to believe and how to behave. However, the child's behavior, to a large extent, is determined by a self-concept that emerges from the way the child thinks parents see him. Even deeply loved children doubt their worth if parents are insensitive, fatigued, pressured by time, guilt-ridden, or willing to allow them to become involved in competition with the other children in the family.

A child needs guidance from his parents, despite the frequent nonchalance and his apparent derision toward what parents say. Though at times parents may be classified as relics of the past, they need to hold with firmness to the basic honesty, decency, and rightness of proper behavior. Mark Twain said that at seventeen he thought his dad was ignorant and stupid and had not been around. At twenty he wondered how the old man had learned so much in three years.

In a "Dear Abby" column the contrast in attitudes was graphically illustrated.

Mother's Love Seems Like Hate

Dear Abby: Will you do me (and countless thousands of teen-aged girls) a tremendous favor and rerun the letter and your reply from your column of September 6, 1968? I wrote it and now I want to write a "P.S." Thank you.

"D"

Dear "D": With pleasure:

Dear Abby: I am a 14 year-old girl and my problem is my mother. I hate her. It may sound terrible to you, but I really hate her. I used to think I would get over it, but now I know I never will.

Sometimes I think I will go out of my mind if she doesn't quit picking on me. I never do anything to suit her. She doesn't like my clothes, my hair, my friends or anything.

My friends are not bums, either. They are good kids and they aren't wild or on pot or anything like that, but my mother says they look like hippies, and they aren't.

Please help me, Abby, before I run away from home. I cry myself to sleep at night because my mother is so hateful. If I babysit, she makes me put the money in the bank. Other girls can buy records or do whatever they want with the money they earn.

Don't tell me to talk to my father. He's always on her side. And don't tell me my mother "loves" me and is only doing things for my own good. If you print my letter, don't sign my name or I'll get killed.

MISERABLE IN PHOENIX

Dear Miserable: **Your letter doesn't shock me at all. I receive many such letters each week. Almost every normal teen-ager alternately loves and hates his parents.**

It's not easy to be criticized, restricted, corrected, and disciplined day in and day out. But parents who really love their children, prove it by consistently letting their children know what is expected of them. Parents who are "soft" and permissive rear confused, insecure children.

I don't expect you to agree with me today, but keep this letter and read it again in three years from now, and then you'll probably understand it perfectly. Good luck, dear. You're lucky. You are loved.

Dear Abby: Now, for my "P.S." I am no longer "Miserable." I am grateful. I am 20 years old, Abby, and I just found that clipping tucked away in my 1968 diary. (I am "cleaning out my closets" because I am going to be married next June, and I'll be moving.)

You were so right. My parents were stricter than the parents of my friends, but now I realize that they set extra high standards for me because they loved me and wanted me to be proud of myself.

I am saving a copy of that clipping to show my daughter if I am ever lucky enough to have one, because I intend to raise my daughter just like my mother raised me, and she may "hate" me for the same reasons I "hated" my mother.

I am graduating from college in June and marrying a wonderful young man on the following Saturday.

How can I thank you?

"D" IN PHOENIX

Dear "D": **You already have. Thanks for writing, Honey, and may all life's blessings be yours.**[7]

Keep Talking

To speak of models and the power of example in the child's life and in shaping his view of the world does not mean that talking is unimportant. Some parents make the mistake of thinking their beliefs will be learned by their example only and do very little discussing of the reasons they believe as they do. Because of this, children from strong homes often seem strangely at sea in knowing what they believe and why they believe it. Sometimes a child comes from a home where parents seem to have every qualification to raise strong children, and yet the child has extraordinary difficulty in choosing standards of conduct or right values.

While it is true that by the time the child becomes an

adolescent he knows what parents believe, many times he still does not know the reason behind these beliefs. Before he simply accepted them. Now he will challenge them to see if he will make them his own. This is the time to make a special effort to keep up communication.

A family inspires and reinforces standards and beliefs by means of conversation. When problems arise or questions are asked, conversation helps evaluate and weigh positions and reactions. As someone has said, "Certainly there will be rules and limits, but the reason behind them develops the teen-ager's standards, not the rule itself."

This is why table conversation and other informal settings in the family, if used rightly, can add much to the teaching of morality within the context of those most concerned.

This is certainly the reason the Scripture speaks of the parents teaching not only at certain scheduled times, but also when getting up, sitting down, walking by the way, and retiring again for the night. This speaks of the continual teaching by example and word that must go on at all times in the home. Blessed is the home that has learned the secret of open, free conversation about any issue. Happy is that adolescent who can put before his parents his deepest questions and have them discussed in love and understanding. Much moral teaching can happen in such an atmosphere.

One of the clearest things learned from research with teen-agers is that they want to know what their parents think on issues more than what any other authority has to say.

If this is true, why is there a breakdown of communication between parents and children? In a survey of over 5,500 high school seniors, only one in ten boys and one in five girls always talked over personal problems with a parent. About half of those queried occasionally shared their problems with their parents, while one in four pointedly stated that they seldom, if ever, took their problems to their parents.

Perhaps part of the reason is shared by one leader of teen-agers. He says neither parents nor teen-agers explain their points of view sufficiently to each other, and the result is that neither "side" understands the other. Their failure to sit down to a calm, clear, complete discussion of differences is often the fault of both sides. Parents are sometimes unwilling to hear and appraise calmly the teen-ager's point of view. Teen-agers suffer from a sense of inadequacy about discussing matters of tension, or they become upset when their arguments are rejected. So in a sense of frustration or anger they just close the door to fuller discussion.

Parents should keep in mind that youth will share to the extent they think their parents can take it. They will also share to the extent that they feel their viewpoint is respected and that they will continue to be loved and accepted after their disclosures.

In short, when young people are treated like adults, by adults, they tend to act like adults. Being listened to does not necessarily mean getting one's own way. A family operates in a healthy way when its members understand that parents, as well as sons or daughters, love one another, accept one another, and make concessions even when they would rather not.

Guiding Principles

1. *Help your adolescent love himself.* This means positive praise. The child who receives no praise at home will respond to the gang that praises and recognizes him in doing wrong. Affirm what the youth does right and recognize and appreciate what he does. Compliment not only good grades but good ideas.

Love means taking time to listen and to do things together. A family in Colorado tried unsuccessfully for years to save enough money to replace their ancient bathroom fixtures with slick modern ones. But each year as skiing time rolled around, it seemed the bathroom money went for a family skiing trip.

Finally, the children were grown and gone. One of the sons recently wrote home, recalling the annual family skiing trips, the good times they had together, and how much he enjoyed them. His father commented, "I can't imagine my son writing and saying, 'Dad, I sure remember our swell bathroom.' "

To help the adolescent have a proper sense of self-love, the parent must seek to use every opportunity possible to build self-esteem.

Dr. Stanley Coopersmith, associate professor of psychology at the Davis campus of the University of California, has done prodigious research to isolate and define the one factor that most successful men and women seem to have in common. It is an attitude of mind called "high self-esteem." The study ran for six years with 1,748 boys, beginning in preadolescence and following the boys through to young manhood. Dr. Coopersmith found that social class, ethnic background, and outside environment played a comparatively minor role in building self-esteem. The child's attitude toward himself was formed within the home. As the mother and father see him, or as he *thinks* they see him, so he tends to see himself. He found that the homes of successful and self-confident persons had these things in common:

First, there was love felt in the family. It was a love expressed in respect and concern for each child. When the child feels he is respected and the object of parental pride, he senses he is a person of significance.

Second, parents of children with high self-esteem were significantly less permissive than were parents of children with low self-esteem. The child in a too-permissive home feels he is not loved enough for parents to care what he does. He also faces undue pressure to make decisions he does not have background or information to make.

Third, there was a marked degree of democracy in the high-self-esteem family. The parents established a code of conduct and life-style, and their own authority within that, yet they encouraged their child to present his own ideas for discussion, even if in disagreement. Opinions were shared and received respectful discussion.

2. *Help the adolescent with struggles of faith and guilt.* A parent dare not belittle the youthful struggle with guilt and faith, but should exercise patience, love, prayer, and understanding. Nor should the parent pretend to be perfect, but rather should share his own doubts as in a mutual search together. The parent's love is ever a symbol of God's abiding love.

3. *Help the adolescent believe he will make it as an adult.* Teens have a fear of the future. The high rate of suicide among teens points to the fear of life. Teens are confronted with all kinds of pressures, such as choosing a career before they understand themselves, and so they require understanding parents who are good sounding boards for their ideas.

One of England's gifted preachers said that when he was a college student he was so wayward and unruly his family unanimously predicted he would go wrong. And he was resentful enough to determine that he would live up to, or down to, their expectation. But one never-to-be-forgotten night, or rather in the early morning hours, as he crept upstairs to his bedroom, shoes in hand, after a night out, a door in the hallway opened, and his grandmother stood there with a lighted candle. She put her hand on his shoulder and said five words, "John, I believe in you." And there in the darkness of his room with no altar but a chair, no ritual but a man making a clean break, the great miracle came to his heart. With someone to believe in him, he came to believe in himself.

4. *Believe that what you have taught the adolescent will have its effect.* This also will create an attitude of accomplishment and hope on the part of the youth.

Ten Simple Commandments

Here are several helpful guides from Marilyn Bonham's *Laughter and Tears of Children:*

Parents are best advised never to sell their children short on love, affection and devotion. The words come easily, but they represent a lifetime of labor of love. And when adolescence does arrive, remember these ten simple commandments

1. Remind yourself often that every one of your children is a person unto him or herself, that they live in different times with constantly shifting standards that may differ from those current when you were a child.

2. Excel in patience toward your teen-age youngster. Listen to him, but don't laugh at him. Don't force your advice down his throat, unless he is willing to listen.

3. Devote more time to encouraging the good in him, less time in punishing the bad.

4. Don't impose qualifications and conditions on your love.

5. Take a good look at yourself. Are you letting your own emotional needs determine those of your children? Are you helping them in their drive for independence? Are you forcing something on them that compensates for something you yourself might have been missing?

6. When conflicts do arise, choose your times and battlegrounds wisely. Try to avoid such conflicts during bedtime, mealtime, weekends, or in public.

7. Do respect his desire for privacy, and keep him informed of family matters.

8. Remember your teen-ager's extreme sensitivities. Be

nice to his friends and make them welcome at home, avoid sarcasm, and stay away from criticism in the presence of them.

9. Enforce discipline and sound rules, but don't insist on dotting the "i" for the sake of "principles." In other words, show some flexibility instead of rigidity.

10. Look ahead and remember that these adolescent difficulties will be memories in a few years hence.[8]

A Letter from Dad

When my son was fifteen years old, I wrote the following letter that may help parents as well as teens:

My dear Son,

It seems strange to write a note to you when we live in the same house. However, we don't get enough time to talk together. Also at times, I feel poor in expressing the love for you which I feel. Then, too, you are not eager to talk many times. I can understand this.

I want to tell you that I love you very much and am proud of you in so many ways. You are in my prayers each day.

You are at the age when, as never before or after, you are becoming a new person. You are now, and will be for the next several years, at the place in life which is called the age of finding one's identity. It is a time of finding out who you are, what you believe, and what you will do with your life. You are moving from childhood dependence to adult independence. This is a necessary stage and it brings many changes. There are great physical changes. You are almost overnight physically mature in many ways. It is a time when you struggle with feelings of self-worth. And it is a good time to realize that you are a special creation of God, different from any other person, with unique qualities, created to make your own special contribution to the world and to all whom you meet.

At your age friends are more important and more influential than at any other time in life. You long for acceptance, especially from those your own age. During the teen years you develop a whole new set of behavioral patterns that will win attraction and approval and can give you poise and ease in social interaction. You will find your own identity largely in relationships to other people and in your response to them and their response to you. This is why the kind of friends you have is so very important.

I know you must be a person in your own right. So you have the urge to be yourself without feeling responsible to those closest to you over the years—your family. Also your personality will develop according to the choices you make and the values that guide your life.

No one can choose your values and standards except you. Your friends will certainly help you choose your values. Your past experience in your family will also help. This is a difficult time for teen-agers and also for parents because you need to test whether the values and standards you have been taught will be your own, or whether you will choose a different set of standards and which ones you will accept or reject.

I know you need opportunities to discover what you will accept or reject. I would not want you to mimic me or be a carbon of me. God created you to be you. I know you need to test whether what you have been taught is the best. This does not mean you must do everything opposite to check which is best. Most things in life can be judged by mere observation. We can see the lives of others and what that kind of living leads to. We can easily see that certain choices lead to a certain kind of existence.

One great danger at this time of life is that to find one's own identity one may thoughtlessly cast aside parents' values and reject parents' standards and uncritically pick up standards and values and morality of a society or other persons of the same age. Many teen-agers accept the standards of fellow teen-agers who are also doing things out of reaction to parents in seeking their own identity. In other words, I'm saying we don't find our own identity and sense of worth by uncritically accepting the standards of someone else, especially if that person is also reacting and inexperienced.

So, my son, I am not surprised that at fifteen you are questioning the values we have tried to live by and which we have tried to teach you. I know you must do this. Your statement the other day regarding God is something you need to think about and come to a conclusion on. To me it seems impossible not to see the evidences of God all around. But I cannot believe in God for you. This is only one example of your search. I can see the difference in lives of those who believe in and seek to obey God and those who don't. But I cannot say you must believe in him and obey him.

Teen-age years are awfully important, therefore, because you are questioning your values and standards, and what you choose determines so much the direction for life. Not that you must decide and have all the answers during the teen years. No, we will always be making choices. But they are some of the most important years of life. And, in questioning the values you grew up with, let me say again, do not toss them aside with little thought for another set of standards someone else puts before you, especially the standards of other inexperienced young people who are also sorting out what they will accept and reject.

As parents we want you to have the needed freedom to decide the values you want to live by. While giving you freedom, we still carry responsibility to place certain limits. The teen-agers who are really insecure and mixed up in our society are the ones who have no limits put upon them. I know also that no caring parent will seek to keep a son or daughter from a helpful and happy experience in life. We want you to be happy in every way. This means that our love seeks to protect you from being hurt and from those experiences that we know bring only grief, sorrow, and suffering.

I know, as I cannot make the final choices for you, so also I cannot be with you everywhere you go. Finally, I cannot prevent you from doing what is wrong and harmful if you desire to do it. God gives each of us all the equipment we need to destroy ourselves if we want to. And regardless what you have been taught and no matter how hard we seek to protect you from evil, yet we, as parents, also realize that you are at the age when you can, by one way or another, turn from it all and even destroy your happiness, now and in the future, by the choice you make. I know we can seek to do the best we know, yet life, *your life,* is in your hands and your future happiness is your decision. Finally, you are responsible, and no one else, for your choices and the results of your choices. Every choice in life, large or small, carries a consequence of good or ill. Whenever we make a choice we also decide a consequence. The Bible calls it the law of sowing and reaping, a law that never changes.

I know that during the teen years relationships are awfully important, especially with those your own age. You will be helped a great deal also by keeping up relationships with persons who have gone through the experiences you are now going through. You will mature as you relate to persons who are more mature and who will challenge your thinking.

We want to be and do all we can for you, Son. No one loves you as much as we do. As I've told many young people, you can always be sure the person who urges you or lets you do wrong of any kind is not really your friend. Such will also drop you any time you are in trouble or in need.

I want to tell you that, regardless of what you do and what choices you make, I will always love you and be ready to help you in every way I can.

Love always,
Dad

Discussion Statements and Questions

1. What particularly in this chapter gave you new understanding of teen-agers?
2. Where did you as a teen-ager feel the greatest strain? Where do you as a parent feel the greatest strain?
3. Discuss Dobson's statement about the danger of attacking the teen-ager's ego.
4. Do you think that physical force should ever be used by a parent in punishing a teen-ager?
5. Discuss the idea of the need for teen-agers to have goals.
6. Do you, in your family, discuss together *why* you act and believe as you do?
7. How much impact does the peer group have on the moral values children accept, particularly during the teen years?
8. Do you think teen-agers today have unique problems that their parents did not face during their teens?
9. Do we play up the identity problem too much today? That is, do we too easily say when teen-agers react that it is simply a stage youth go through in finding their identity?
10. If you were writing a letter to your teen-ager, what things would you include?

Appendix

Understanding Age Growth

This chart seeks to summarize some of the characteristics which the majority of youth experience. Resources for this material include the Minnesota Department of Health, as well as the writings of Dr. Arnold Gesell, Dr. Kent Gelbert, Dr. Frances L. Ilg, Dr. Milton I. Levine, John Leuellen, and Willard C. Olson.

Reprinted by permission from *Sex Education*, Approach/Program/Resources/For the parish. Copyright 1968. Sacred Design Associates, Inc., 840 Colorado Avenue, So., Minneapolis, Minnesota 55416.

	PHYSICAL	SOCIAL	SPIRITUAL	SEXUAL
AGE 5 Kindergarten	Child can run, jump, climb. Learns to hop and skip this year. Child grows approximately 6 inches and gains about 10 pounds in weight. Can dress self, tie shoes, brush teeth, button clothes. Gains reading readiness.	Children learn to relate to others outside the home. Activity with others is very important at this age. Children should learn give and take in preparation for life. The child likes to be at home with mother, or to know she is near.	Accepts fact of God as Creator and loving Father. Sometimes confuses names and persons of God and Jesus. At times worries over ideas that God sees everything he does. Likes stories from the Bible. Usually enjoys being in the church school class.	Child is usually curious about "where he came from." Asks many questions about babies. Is curious about the difference between male and female. Family unit is good beginning for basic sex information, which should be gradually progressive at each succeeding age.

ington, D.C.: United States Catholic Conference, 1976.

Raths, Louis et al. *Values and Teaching: Working with Values in the Classroom.* Columbus: Charles E. Merrill Publishing Co., 1966.

Rokeach, Milton. *Beliefs, Attitudes and Values: A Theory of Organization and Change.* San Francisco: Jossey-Bass, 1968.

―――. *The Nature of Human Values.* New York: The Free Press, 1973.

Saltzstein, Herbert D. "Social Development and Moral Development: A Perspective on the Role of Parents and Peers." In *Moral Development and Behavior,* edited by T. Lickona. New York: Holt, Rinehart and Winston, 1976.

Stewart, Charles William. *Adolescent Religion: A Developmental Study of the Religion of Youth.* Nashville: Abingdon, 1967.

Strommen, Merton P. et al. *Study of Generations: Report of a Two-Year Study of 5000 Lutherans Between the Ages of 15 & 65, Their Beliefs, Values, Attitudes, Behavior.* Minneapolis: Augsburg Publishing House, 1972.

Thibodeau, Lynn. *The Tall Young Strangers.* New York: Carillon Books, 1977.

Thompson, Andrew D. *When Your Child Learns to Choose.* St. Meinrad, Ind.: Abbey Press, 1978.

Thompson, W. Faliaferro. *An Adventure in Love.* Atlanta: John Knox Press, 1962.

―――. *Adventure in Parenthood.* Atlanta: John Knox Press, 1961.

Turiel, Eliot. "Conflicts and Transition in Adolescent Moral Development." *Child Development* 45, 1974.

Werner, Hazen G. *Look at the Family Now.* Nashville: Abingdon, 1970.

White, Burton L. *The First Three Years of Life.* Englewood Cliffs, N.J.: Prentice-Hall, 1975.

Wickes, Frances G. *The Inner World of Childhood.* Englewood Cliffs, N.J.: Prentice-Hall, 1966.

Winter, Gibson. *Love and Conflict: New Patterns in Family Life.* Garden City, N.Y.: Doubleday & Co., 1958.

Wolf, Anna W. M. *Your Child's Emotional Health.* Public Affairs Pamphlet No. 264.

Wright, Derek. *The Psychology of Moral Behaviour.* Gannon.

Yankelovich, Skelly, and White, Inc. General Mills American Family Report, 1976-77, *Raising Children in a Changing Society.* New York: General Mills, Inc., 1977.

Young, Leontine. *Life Among the Giants.* New York: McGraw-Hill Book Co., 1966.

Youniss, James. "Another Perspective on Social Cognition." In *Minnesota Symposia on Child Psychology, Vol. 9,* edited by A. Pick. Minneapolis: University of Minnesota Press, 1975.